# WOULD YOU RATHER
# CHRISTMAS
# EDITION

Silly & Hilarious Questions For
Kids, Teens & Adults

# GAME BOOK

# HOW TO PLAY

Would You Rather is a game where you're faced with two scenarios, and you have to choose only one.

One person asks the question, and the other person can discuss their answer to question before choosing between them.

Making a choice can feel impossible!

You'll have lots of fun as you ponder the silly questions and make your challenging choice.

There's only one rule in the 'Would you Rather' game, and that is, have fun!

# INDEX OF QUESTIONS

# WOULD YOU RATHER ...

wake up to find you had grown a white Santa beard or discover you had grown a pair of reindeer antlers?

open your gift and find a dead mouse inside or find a live mouse living under your Christmas tree?

# WOULD YOU RATHER ...

bite into a mince pie and
find a dead worm inside
or bite into a mince pie and
find a live worm inside?

have to go to bed
very early on Christmas Eve
or stay in bed until
lunchtime on Christmas Day?

# WOULD YOU RATHER ...

wear your new Christmas
socks every day for a month
or sleep for one night
in a bed of fleas?

be as small and cute
as an elf
or as furry and fast
as a reindeer?

# WOULD YOU RATHER ...

forget to bring your
Secret Santa gift
or find that Secret Santa
has forgotten your gift?

have every day be
Christmas Eve
or have every day
be Boxing Day?

# WOULD YOU RATHER ...

chop firewood
to put on the fire
OR bake cookies
to eat in front of the fire?

have icicles
instead of a nose
OR have jingle bells
instead of ears?

# WOULD YOU RATHER ...

sing
a Christmas song
or dance
a Christmas dance?

laugh until
you're sick
or eat sweets
until you're sick?

# WOULD YOU RATHER ...

give away half of
your presents to charity
or give away half of your
clothes to charity?

go to church
on Christmas Day
or have a lie-in
until midday?

# WOULD YOU RATHER ...

have fun but
be on the naughty list
or be on
Santa's good list?

help out in a
homeless shelter
or have to clean your house
from top to bottom?

# WOULD YOU RATHER ...

work extra hard and finish
at lunchtime on Christmas Eve
or play games and go home
at the normal time?

make a gift for your
teacher and /or boss,
or buy a gift
for your teacher / boss?

14

# WOULD YOU RATHER ...

open gifts at
midnight
OR open gifts
at dawn?

drive around looking at all
the Christmas lights
OR have snow fall
on Christmas Day?

# WOULD YOU RATHER ...

decorate the
Christmas tree
or make and decorate a
gingerbread house?

Roast chestnuts
by an open fire
or kiss someone
under the mistletoe?

# WOULD YOU RATHER ...

eat an overcooked
Brussels sprout
or eat a spoonful
of brandy butter?

have to do the
washing up
or have to put
the plates away?

# WOULD YOU RATHER ...

eat an
overcooked turkey
or eat an
undercooked goose?

have a Christmas cake
filled with fruit
or a Christmas cake
made of chocolate?

# WOULD YOU RATHER ...

spill fizzy drink on
the new sofa
or spill gravy on
the new carpet?

sneeze into your
neighbor's lunch
or have your neighbor
sneeze on your lunch?

# WOULD YOU RATHER ...

have a yukky dinner and a
delicious dessert,
or a yukky dessert
and a lovely dinner?

eat a stale
mince pie with custard
or eat a dry piece of
Christmas cake with cream?

# WOULD YOU RATHER ...

eat your turkey with
lashings of cream
or eat your Christmas pud
with lashings of gravy?

enjoy poolside cocktails
by the pool on Christmas Day
or enjoy drinking hot
chocolate in a remote cabin?

# WOULD YOU RATHER ...

drink so much
fizzy drink that you're sick
or eat so much candy
that you're sick?

eat curled up turkey
sandwiches or eat stale,
soggy crisps/chips?

# WOULD YOU RATHER ...

eat your own
bogey
or eat a
Brussels sprout?

make the perfect
Christmas cookie
or cook the perfect
Christmas dinner?

# WOULD YOU RATHER ...

drink a hot chocolate with
whipped cream every day
or eat a hot mince pie
with custard every day?

be given a bag of
chocolate coins
or a bag of
foreign coins?

# WOULD YOU RATHER ...

eat turkey-flavored
popcorn
or eat fish-flavor
ice cream?

invite your teacher/boss
to Christmas dinner
or have a soggy kiss on
the lips from your aunt?

# WOULD YOU RATHER ...

eat maggot
flavor chocolates
or eat
chocolate-coated maggots?

eat a mince pie
filled with crushed snails
or eat a mince pie
filled with squished frogs?

# WOULD YOU RATHER ...

have a stocking filled
with your favorite candy
or have a stocking filled
by your favorite person?

have one Christmas gift
chosen by a stranger
or five gifts chosen by
your nearest & dearest?

# WOULD YOU RATHER ...

wear an ugly sweater
from Great Aunt Agatha
or play dominoes
with your annoying cousins?

buy your Christmas gifts
at the local shops
or shop
for them online?

# WOULD YOU RATHER ...

wake up and see
Santa and his Reindeer
OR eat the tasty treats
you left out for him?

open your gifs
in just a few minutes
OR spread out opening
your gifts through the day?

# WOULD YOU RATHER ...

get a boring pair of socks
as a gift
or get a book that you've
already read as a gift?

get a gift that you put on
your wish list weeks ago
or get a surprise gift
that's really amazing?

# WOULD YOU RATHER ...

tidy up & recycle
all the used wrapping paper
or clear away the dishes
after Christmas dinner?

be a Christmas gift that
gets played with and broken
or be a gift that's admired
and put on the shelf?

# WOULD YOU RATHER ...

wake up to discover
it's Christmas Day
or wake up to discover
it's your birthday?

Receive a year's
supply of chocolate
or have a year with
no homework?

# WOULD YOU RATHER ...

give two meaningful
gifts to family
or give ninety nine gifts
to people you don't know?

wrap all your Christmas
gifts yourself
or have a gift-wrapping
service wrap them for you?

# WOULD YOU RATHER ...

Christmas preparations started in September or that preparations started on Christmas Eve?

the shops stopped playing Christmas music or stopped putting up Christmas decorations?

# WOULD YOU RATHER ...

be given a puppy
with no tail
OR a kitten with
no ears?

travel to Disneyland
on Christmas Day
OR stay at home
with your family?

# WOULD YOU RATHER ...

Receive a gift of
poo-smelling body spray
or receive a gift of
vomit-tasting lip balm?

sneak down in the night
and open all your gifts
or open your gifts
with all the family?

# WOULD YOU RATHER ...

be the joke inside
the Christmas cracker
or be the paper hat
sat on Grandma's head?

go outside and
build a snowman
or go outside
and go sledging?

# WOULD YOU RATHER ...

sing a Christmas Carol
to complete strangers
or have complete strangers
sing Christmas Carols to you?

find a tarantula spider
inside your cracker
or find a slug
hidden in your sprouts?

# WOULD YOU RATHER ...

live in the North Pole
and it always be winter
or live in a straw shack
and it always be summer?

live in
a chocolate house
or live in
a candy house?

# WOULD YOU RATHER ...

watch the Christmas parade or be in the Christmas parade?

change your name to Ebenezer or change your name to Jesus?

# WOULD YOU RATHER ...

spend Christmas
in the North Pole
or spend Christmas
in Bethlehem?

wear a Christmas sweater
with a reindeer face on it
or wear Grandma's
jumper from last year?

# WOULD YOU RATHER ...

bake cookies and
give them all away
or decorate cookies and
eat them all yourself?

buy something new
to give as a gift
or give someone the gift
you were given last year?

# WOULD YOU RATHER ...

spend an hour
wrapping Christmas gifts
or spend an hour
writing Christmas cards?

spend five minutes
writing a thank you card
or spend ten minutes saying
thank you on the phone?

# WOULD YOU RATHER ...

have a chocolate advent calendar you have to share or have an advent calendar with pictures, but no chocolate?

give away one of your gifts as a random act of kindness or buy a gift to give away as a random act of kindness?

# WOULD YOU RATHER ...

be the angel sitting at the top of the Christmas tree OR be the flashing Christmas tree lights?

be a Christmas tree sitting in a family home OR be a Christmas tree standing in a Swedish forest?

# WOULD YOU RATHER ...

have silver
tinsel for hair
or have Christmas
baubles for eyes?

have a giant Snowman
in your garden
or a giant Christmas tree
in your home?

# WOULD YOU RATHER ...

Christmas decorations were in shops before Halloween or that decorations weren't in shops until 1st December?

have a real tree that you choose each year or have the same artificial tree every year?

# WOULD YOU RATHER ...

wear a Christmas hat
that's too big
or wear a Christmas hat
that's too small?

go for a walk
on Christmas Day
or have a snowball fight
on Christmas Day?

# WOULD YOU RATHER ...

help to decorate
the Christmas tree
or come home to discover the
tree is already decorated?

wear a Christmas outfit
made out of tinsel
or wear an outfit made out
of wrapping paper?

# WOULD YOU RATHER ...

pick prickly
holly branches
or cut ivy
away from a tree?

write and receive
100 Christmas cards
or write and receive
10 Christmas cards?

# WOULD YOU RATHER ...

eat turkey
for three days
or eat pizza
for three days?

be able to sing in
the Christmas talent show
or be able to dance in
the Christmas talent show?

# WOULD YOU RATHER ...

have one CRACKER with
an amazing gift inside
OR have ten CRACKERS with
rubbish gifts and Riddles?

you Rather sing
Christmas Carols
OR sing
Frosty the Snowman?

# WOULD YOU RATHER ...

have one
big present
or have
ten small presents?

eat turkey
for Christmas dinner
or eat turkey pizza
for Christmas dinner?

# WOULD YOU RATHER ...

leave Santa
a glass of milk
OR leave Santa
a glass of whisky?

know what gifts
you're going to get
OR have all your gifts
as big surprises?

# WOULD YOU RATHER ...

wake up to discover it was the Christmas vacation OR wake up to discover you were on summer vacation?

go to school OR work and be the only one wearing a Christmas sweater
OR be the only one NOT wearing a Christmas sweater?

# WOULD YOU RATHER ...

would you rather play a board game with family and win or an play online game with friends and lose?

leave your favorite chocolate treat for Santa or eat your favorite chocolate treat yourself?

# WOULD YOU RATHER ...

get the gift that was meant
for your mum
or get the gift that was
meant for your dad?

have five
drummers drumming
or have six
geese a-laying??

# WOULD YOU RATHER ...

would you rather never
hear Christmas music again
or never see
Christmas decorations again?

have to kiss your
aunt under the mistletoe
or kiss a stranger under
the mistletoe?

# WOULD YOU RATHER ...

be a fart trapped
inside a tummy
or the escaped air
polluting the room?

wear a Christmas jumper
in July
or wear a tshirt
in December?

# WOULD YOU RATHER ...

have a bright, red shiny nose
like Rudolf
or have a carrot for a nose
like Frosty the Snowman?

have a burp that
tastes of sprouts
or have a burp that
tastes of turkey?

# WOULD YOU RATHER ...

be covered in
reindeer poo
or be covered
in reindeer snot?

have to hide a sprout
under your armpit
or hide a carrot
in your sock?

# WOULD YOU RATHER ...

have your wee
smell of Brussels sprouts
or have your poo come out
like rabbit droppings?

scare someone by wrapping
a spider inside their gift
or scare someone
by jumping out at them?

# WOULD YOU RATHER ...

have a Rotten cold
at Christmas
OR have a power cut
on Christmas Day?

laugh at someone else's joke
OR have someone else
laugh at your joke?

# WOULD YOU RATHER ...

wear green
elf tights
or have a nose that lights up
every time you speak?

need the toilet for a long poo
during Christmas dinner
or need a poo just as
it's time to open presents?

# WOULD YOU RATHER ...

spend Christmas
playing in the snow
or spend your summer
vacation swimming in the sea?

eat one hundred
mince pies
or eat one hundred
carrots?

# WOULD YOU RATHER ...

have to change
a baby's nappy
or clear up a
dog's poo?

share your most embarrassing
family Christmas tradition
or tell everyone which gift
you disliked most?

# WOULD YOU RATHER ...

put your head inside
the Christmas pudding
or put your head
inside the turkey's bottom?

walk across a floor
covered in holly
or walk across a floor
covered in chestnuts?

# WOULD YOU RATHER ...

have runny eggnog poured over your face or have reindeer snot poured on your hair?

be trapped inside the body of one of Santa's elves or trapped inside the body of a flying reindeer?

# WOULD YOU RATHER ...

fReeze in an ice bath
at the NoRth Pole
oR bake in the sun on Santa's
sleigh as flies acRoss AfRica?

be given a
box of spideRs
oR be given a
bucket of snakes?

# WOULD YOU RATHER ...

get to sit
on Santa's lap
or get to ride
on Santa's sleigh?

have to eat
ten candy canes
or have to eat
one Brussels sprout?

# WOULD YOU RATHER ...

it was the day after
Christmas every day
OR that it was
Christmas Eve every day?

wake up to discover you've
turned into your mother
OR wake up to discover
you've turned into your dad?

# WOULD YOU RATHER ...

have custard
poured all over you
or have cream
poured all over you?

eat cookies
until you feel sick
or eat chocolate
until you feel sick?

# WOULD YOU RATHER ...

star in the
Christmas nativity
or dress up as your
favorite cartoon character?

meet the Grinch
on a dark Christmas night
or meet Ebeneezer Scrooge
on a dark Christmas night?

# WOULD YOU RATHER ...

be Tiny Tim
in A Christmas Carol
or be
Ebenezer Scrooge?

be visited by the
Ghost of Christmas Past
or be visited by the
Ghost of Christmas Future?

# WOULD YOU RATHER ...

watch your family's favorite
Christmas movie on repeat
or bang your head
against a brick wall?

watch Christmas movies
all year round
or never watch another
Christmas movie again?

# WOULD YOU RATHER ...

wake up to discover
you've turned into an elf
or wake up to discover
you've turned into a reindeer?

watch a vintage black &
white Christmas movie
or watch your
favorite cartoon?

# WOULD YOU RATHER ...

spend Christmas in the world
of Little Women
or live in the era
of A Christmas Carol?

be Buddy
the Elf
or be the little boy
in The Polar Express?

# WOULD YOU RATHER ...

sing along to
White Christmas
or sing along to
Walking In The Air?

hum along to
Silent Night
or hum along
Away in a Manger?

# WOULD YOU RATHER ...

star in a Remake
of Home Alone
oR star in a Remake
of PolaR ExpRess?

watch a Romantic movie
on Christmas Day
oR watch a scary movie
on Christmas Day?

# WOULD YOU RATHER ...

star as Santa Claus
in a Christmas movie
or star as a ghost
in a Christmas movie?

go to the cinema to see
this year's Christmas movie
or go to the theatre
to see a Christmas musical?

# WOULD YOU RATHER ...

would you Rather stay in watching home movies or have friends round and play party games?

would you Rather your TV blew up on Christmas Day or your heating stopped working on Christmas Day?

# WOULD YOU RATHER ...

be the stockings
hanging above the fireplace
or be the baubles hanging
on the Christmas tree?

sit and read by the fire
with only candlelight to see by
or sit alone and watch
the TV all night?

# WOULD YOU RATHER ...

watch the movie
It's A Wonderful Life
or watch the movie
Miracle on 34th Street?

watch The Muppet
Christmas Carol or
watch Holiday Inn
with Bing Crosby?

# WOULD YOU RATHER ...

sing with
Bing Crosby
or dance with
Fred Astaire?

be Santa in the
Christmas Parade
or be the rock star with a
Christmas number One?

# WRITE YOUR OWN
# WOULD YOU RATHER ...

?

?

# WRITE YOUR OWN
# WOULD YOU RATHER ...

?

?

# WRITE YOUR OWN
# WOULD YOU RATHER ...

?

?

# WRITE YOUR OWN
# WOULD YOU RATHER ...

?

?

# WRITE YOUR OWN
# WOULD YOU RATHER ...

?

?

# WOULD YOU RATHER ...

Other books by Archie Brain include:

Would You Rather - Travel Edition - a great boredom buster for long car rides, road trips or plane journeys.

It's filled with silly and fun questions to ask your family and friends!

## Coming Soon:

Would You Rather Easter Edition

Would You Rather Disgusting & Gross Edition

Would You Rather Zombie Apocalypse Edition

Follow Archie Brain on Amazon to be notified of new releases!

Made in the USA
Las Vegas, NV
09 December 2024

13738189R00050